A TICK-BORNE PLAGUE

Lyme disease is the most common bug-borne disease in the United States. If diagnosed and treated early in an otherwise healthy individual, it may be no worse than a bout of the flu. However, because of the difficulties of accurate diagnosis and the impaired immune systems of many of its victims, a neglected Lyme infection can result in serious complications affecting the heart, the joints, the brain, and the nervous system. Moreover, the traditional "cure," heavy-duty antibiotic therapy, can cause debilitating side effects.

This invaluable booklet, written by a leading doctor of nutritional medicine, tells you everything you need to know to protect yourself from this dreaded infection. Dr. Hoffman describes the course of the disease, standard diagnostic procedures, and treatment options. Most important, he discusses the specific nutrients, vitamins, and minerals that can rebuild the immune system and soften the effects of antibiotic therapy.

ABOUT THE AUTHOR

Ronald L. Hoffman, M.D., is Medical Director of The Hoffman Center for Holistic Medicine in New York City. A graduate of Albert Einstein College of Medicine, he is a Diplomate of the American College for Advancement of Medicine and The American Academy of Environmental Medicine. He is the author of *The Diet-Type Weight Loss Program, Seven Weeks to a Settled Stomach,* and *Tired All the Time: How to Regain Your Lost Energy.* He also hosts "Health Talk," a daily radio program in the New York area.

LYME DISEASE

HOW TO AVOID, DETECT AND TREAT THIS DANGEROUS TICK-BORNE PLAGUE

Ronald L. Hoffman, M.D.

Keats Publishing, Inc. New Canaan, Connecticut

LYME DISEASE

Copyright © 1994 by Ronald L. Hoffman

ISBN: 0-87983-617-2

Printed in the United States of America

Good Health Guides are published by
Keats Publishing, Inc.
27 Pine Street (Box 876)
New Canaan, Connecticut 06840-0876

Contents

Figure 1

Lyme Disease Case Reports, 1992
from THE CENTER FOR DISEASE CONTROL

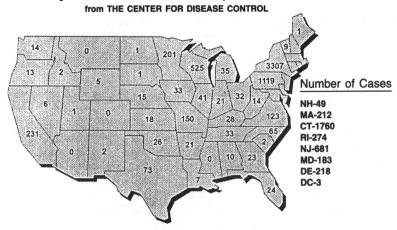

Number of Cases

NH-49
MA-212
CT-1760
RI-274
NJ-681
MD-183
DE-218
DC-3

Figure 2

DEER TICKS
(actual size, not engorged)

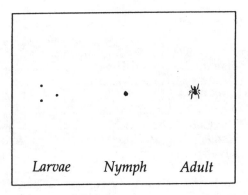

Larvae   Nymph   Adult

INTRODUCTION: A DETECTIVE STORY

Since the mid-1960s, Polly Murray, a mother of four living in Old Lyme, Conn., hadn't been feeling at all well. She suffered from rashes, headaches, swollen joints, muscle stiffness, and overwhelming tiredness. Over a period of ten years, she saw a number of doctors, none of whom were able to help her. Many of them diagnosed her problems as psychosomatic, and recommended that she see a psychiatrist. But by 1975, her whole family had fallen ill: Her older son had developed facial palsy, her husband was on crutches because of painful, swollen knees, and her two younger sons had the same swollen, inflamed knee joints. Then one of the boys was diagnosed with juvenile rheumatoid arthritis, a rare autoimmune disease that strikes about five children in 100,000. Polly called the State Health Department, but they could not make sense of the strange mix of symptoms. However, one of Polly's friends, Judy Mensch, was aware that four other children in the same area had been diagnosed with this rare disease, and that nearly twenty were suffering from similar problems. When Judy called the State Health Department to report this strange statistical aberration, the Department swung into action.

Dr. Allen C. Steere, a rheumatologist from Yale-New Haven Hospital, was called in to investigate. Within a year, Dr. Steere had discovered more than fifty cases of related illness within the small community of Lyme, perched beside the Connecticut River. Many suffered from arthritis and painful, swollen joints, or from headaches and neurological symptoms. About one quarter of them remembered having a strange rash, shaped like a bulls-eye, with a raised, red ring and a clear center, at about the time their symptoms began. Since the cause of the illness was as yet unknown, Dr. Steere and his colleagues called it simply, Lyme disease.

Still, there was a suspect. The rash reminded Dr. Steere of the rash caused by the bite of the sheep tick in Europe, which had been observed since 1900, especially in Scandinavia. Within a few years, Dr. Steere saw several new patients who remembered being bitten by a tick, and one of them had saved the tick. It was a deer tick, of the species *Ixodes dammini*, and it turned out that this kind of tick was about thirty times more prevalent in the area around Lyme, where the illness was rampant, than on the other side of the Connecticut River.

Steere and others suspected that the deer tick (which is much smaller than the common dog tick) was transmitting some kind of virus or infectious agent. But it was not until 1982 that Dr. Willy Burgdorfer, a leading authority on ticks, discovered the corkscrew-shaped bacteria, of the type called spirochetes, in the bodies of deer ticks collected on Shelter Island, where Lyme disease was also rampant. The spirochete was subsequently named *Borrelia burgdorferi*, after its discoverer. And sure enough, the bacteria were found in the rashes, and in the blood and spinal fluid of Lyme disease patients.

WHAT IS LYME DISEASE?

Lyme disease is a complex, potentially dangerous, and potentially chronic illness that begins with infection by the *Borrelia* bacterium, which is transmitted by several species of ticks to animals and people. The initial infection can cause flu-like symptoms, including headache, sore throat, stiff neck, fever, muscle aches, fatigue, and general malaise. In 25 percent or more of cases, there is a typical bulls-eye rash, with a raised, swollen reddish ring that expands outward from the tick bite. This rash is unique to Lyme disease. If diagnosed early, the infection can be treated with a course of antibiotics, and no further symptoms will appear. Some people seem to overcome the initial infection, even if not treated, and develop no further complications.

However, Lyme disease poses two special risks. First, the initial infection may evade diagnosis. The ticks that transmit the disease are easily missed, since they may be no larger than a poppy seed, or the period at the end of this sentence, and the bite is not painful. The characteristic rash occurs in only one quarter of cases, and the initial symptoms resemble flu or a passing viral infection, and generally subside on their own, whether treated or not.

Second, if it is not diagnosed and treated early (within weeks or months), the infection can result in serious complications. Advanced Lyme disease can affect the heart, the joints, the brain, and the nervous system and cause serious, life-disrupting and painful illness that is difficult to diagnose, difficult to treat, and sometimes evades cure altogether. The initial symptoms of infection with Lyme disease generally subside within a few weeks. But weeks or months later, new, unrelated symptoms may appear, including arthritis, heart problems, facial palsy, muscle pain, extreme fatigue, headaches, memory loss, and depression. These symptoms can be intermittent, lasting from a few days to several months, and disappearing for long periods of time. In chronic cases they can last for years. Symptoms may switch from one part of the body to another, shifting from joint to joint, from muscle pain to headaches and neurological symptoms. They can mimic a variety of other illnesses, from rheumatoid arthritis to multiple sclerosis. Unfortunately, there is no definitive test to establish the presence of Lyme disease. There is a blood test that measures the reaction of the immune system to the *Borrelia* spirochete, but results are often inconclusive, and can show up as negative even in people who have the disease. The variety of symptoms, and the lack of a positive blood test, can make advanced stages of the disease quite difficult to diagnose.

Advanced Lyme disease is treated with a long course of antibiotics, sometimes administered intravenously over a period of months. Some people seem to develop chronic symptoms, especially painful arthritis and profound fatigue, that recur even after extended treatment.

Since its discovery in the 1970s, reported cases of Lyme disease have increased dramatically, from a few hundred cases to over 10,000 per year in the United States. The disease is found all over the world, on every continent except Antarctica, but is most common in Northern Europe, especially Germany and Scandinavia, and in North America. Cases of Lyme disease have been reported in 43 states, but most occur in the Northeast, in states along the Atlantic coast from Pennsylvania to Maine; in the upper Midwest, especially Wisconsin and Minnesota; and in the Pacific Northwest, from northern California to Washington. Seventy-seven percent of cases in the United States are reported in five states: New York, Connecticut, Pennsylvania, New Jersey, and Wisconsin. Lyme disease is now the most common bug-borne disease in the United States, and a number of hospitals and clinics have set up specialized facilities for research, diagnosis, and treatment. (See Figure 1, page vi.)

The difficulties of diagnosis, and the debilitating effects of advanced Lyme disease, have combined to make it a controversial, problematic illness. Anxiety surrounds the subject. Public health information, and scare stories in the press, have terrified many who live in the endemic areas. Those with long-term, debilitating disease have to deal with the anxieties of a difficult diagnosis, shifting symptoms, and controversies over treatment. Paradoxically, Lyme disease is probably both over-diagnosed and under-diagnosed. Many patients become convinced they have it but don't, and others who do have it may be told they don't. Patients with Lyme disease have had their symptoms ascribed to everything from chronic fatigue syndrome (CFS) to Alzheimer's disease to psychiatric problems, and have gone for years without satisfactory treatment. At the same time, there are patients, and some doctors, who jump to a diagnosis of Lyme disease without carefully ruling out other illnesses with similar symptoms, and who proceed too quickly to costly, long-term antibiotic treatment that has its own considerable risks.

The fact is, medical knowledge about Lyme disease is still "under development." Doctors and researchers are making new discoveries each year in the areas of diagnosis, testing, treatment, and prevention. While there are clear-cut cases that can be easily diagnosed and treated, advanced Lyme disease can be difficult to diagnose and treat. In such cases, anyone who is looking at a possible diagnosis of Lyme disease should approach the subject in a calm, rational way. It's best to work with a doctor who has had some experience with the illness and can make a thorough, detailed evaluation, carefully considering both symptoms and medical history. This could be a medical specialist, perhaps a rheumatologist or infectious disease specialist, or even a general practitioner who may work in an endemic area and may have much experience with the disease. An experienced doctor should be able to distinguish Lyme disease from other diseases with similar symptoms, and to evaluate the possibility of a "mixed illness"—Lyme disease combined with other ailments.

In this booklet, we'll provide the essential information needed to understand how Lyme disease is currently diagnosed, treated, and—perhaps most important of all—prevented. First, let's look at a simple, clear-cut diagnosis and a successful treatment.

DIAGNOSIS AND CURE: THE HOLISTIC APPROACH

Joe was a high school junior who lived across the river from Manhattan in Queens, New York. He was an honors student, and a dedicated athlete, working out regularly and building up his physique for the wrestling team. At sixteen, he had a terrific appetite, and was still growing, gaining weight and bulking up from his workouts. Joe and his family spent their summers in Montauk, out at the tip of Long Island, enjoying the seashore. One November, his parents called me, distraught. About halfway through the fall semester, Joe had begun to develop achy muscles and joints, and was feeling profoundly tired all the time, and psychologically pretty "down" as well. He'd lost his appetite, and was actually losing weight. By the time he came to me, he didn't look well, certainly not like the high-energy, athletic teenager his parents had described.

I thought about the sudden change in his health after his summer in Montauk, which is a known Lyme disease "hot spot," and about his achy joints. Both were a tip-off to possible Lyme disease, so I asked him if he'd noticed the characteristic rash, with the reddish circle and blanched interior. And sure enough, he remembered having several rashes like that after a canoe trip through the tidal marshes that summer. But they had gone away and he'd thought nothing more of it. I sent him to a reliable university hospital for the antibody blood test, and sure enough he had very high Lyme disease indicators. At this point, it was probably at least three months after his exposure, and maybe a month since his secondary symptoms had begun. I started him on antibiotic treatment with no further ado, and reassured his parents that he would do fine.

However, I did not rely solely on antibiotics in treating Joe. Antibiotics can "put out the fire," but they do not restore the body to health. In fact, antibiotics can present their own challenges to health, and in some cases an antibiotic "cure" can leave a patient in worse health than before treatment. With Lyme disease, as with many other kinds of illness, it's important to treat the whole body, and the whole patient. We can't just rely on a drug to restore someone to health, especially after a long and debilitating course of illness.

Since Lyme disease presents a severe challenge to the system, I talked to Joe about his diet and lifestyle, and also prescribed a protocol of vitamins and nutrients to support his recovery. Joe was already an active, athletic teenager, so I didn't have to worry too much about his desire to get back to his program of sports and exercise. But I did talk to him about diet. I took this opportunity to encourage a good natural diet, free of the sugar, caffeine, high-fat foods, and sometimes alcohol, that make up the typical teenager's diet. I encouraged a diet including lean protein, essential oils, whole grains, and lots of green leafy vegetables.

Antibiotic treatment can kill off some of the natural, beneficial bacteria that live in the digestive tract. In their absence, the yeast organism called *Candida* can proliferate and take over, causing a whole range of symptoms, including fatigue, gas, bloating, diarrhea, and frequent vaginal infections in women. To keep Joe from developing a yeast infection, I prescribed several measures. First, I recommended a daily serving of unsweetened yogurt, with live acidophilus culture, or acidophilus capsules as a substitute. Acidophilus, one of the beneficial bacteria that naturally lives in the gut, can help in keeping yeast growth under control. Second, I warned Joe against the foods that can cause yeast growth, especially sugars and refined carbohydrates, including cookies, cakes, candy, ice cream, soda, and natural sweeteners including fructose, malt, barley and fruit juice. And I told him to steer clear of yeast-containing foods such as breads, baked goods, cheese, mushrooms, vinegar, soy sauce and fermented foods such as olives and pickles.

To help restore Joe to health, I also put him on a program of vitamin and nutrient supplements. As a kind of a helpful "jump start," I gave him an initial series of intravenous vitamin C treatments to enhance tissue repair. I then prescribed a multivitamin, with additional supplements of oral vitamin C and zinc. Vitamin C supplements can be of great benefit in fighting the effects of infections like Lyme disease.

I also recommended a zinc supplement, because zinc is immune-stimulating, and helps restore normal taste sensation and normal physical growth. Zinc is especially important for growing children and adolescents, and is helpful in restoring appetite. Actually, adolescent males have the highest zinc requirements, so this was a key nutrient for Joe, who'd been losing weight instead of gaining.

After three weeks of holistic and antibiotic treatment, Joe experienced an amazing improvement in his joint pain. His energy levels started to climb, the feelings of malaise disappeared, his appetite returned, and he began to gain weight again. I kept him on antibiotics for an additional three weeks as a precaution, to make sure the *Borrelia* spirochete was completely eradicated. And I made sure he maintained his healthy diet and kept up with the vitamins and nutrients. He came back three months later, looking much better, and by his six-month checkup he'd gained a total of twenty pounds, mostly in lean body mass, and looked like the active athlete he had been. At this point, I did order another blood test, and the antibody levels had gone way down. Though the antibody test is not an absolutely reliable indicator that Lyme disease is out of the system, his symptoms had clearly vanished, his health had returned, and he was obviously cured.

Joe's was a very straightforward case, both in diagnosis and treatment. Here we had a Lyme infection of relatively short duration, in a young man with a robust immune system. Joe had a classical response to the infection, with the primary symptom of the target rash and the secondary symptom of achy joints. And he had a clear-cut response to antibiotic treatment and natural therapy. (Several months had elapsed between his infection and the secondary symptoms, but the six-week course of antibiotics, along with the natural therapy, was effective in completely wiping out his symptoms, with no relapse thereafter.)

I should point out that six weeks is a rather long course of antibiotics, and I would not recommend it for most infections. I am very concerned about the overuse of antibiotics, and the risks of inducing secondary infections like yeast infection and engendering microbes with multiple resistance to antibiotics. However, the seven-to-ten-day course that is prescribed for most types of infections is just not enough to wipe out the Lyme spirochete and prevent relapses. This is because the Lyme spirochete takes up residence deep in tissue, in cerebrospinal fluid, and even within cells, in places where it's hard for antibiotics to reach. So we have to bend our normal practice here. And this is all the more reason why we have to support recovery in a holistic way, using diet and nutrients to prevent the side effects of antibiotic treatment as they restore the whole body to health.

HOW LYME DISEASE IS TRANSMITTED: TICKS AND OTHER CARRIERS

The tick first identified as the transmitter of Lyme disease in the Northeast, *Ixodes dammini*, is known as the "deer tick" because in its adult stage it lives and mates on the white-tailed deer. However, "deer tick" may be something of a misnomer, since the tick lives and feeds on many other animals—including wild animals like field mice, opossums and raccoons, and domestic animals and pets like dogs, horses, and cattle. In fact, it's been found on at least 30 different species of mammals, 49 species of birds, and several reptiles. In earlier stages of their life cycle, the ticks hitch a ride on the smaller animals, especially field mice, and then fall off onto grasses and brush, and wait to catch their next ride (and meal) on larger animals like dogs, deer, and people. Lyme disease has been spreading steadily over recent years in a southerly direction, and it's thought that the tick is hitching a ride on migratory birds.

In different parts of the country, different ticks carry the disease. In the Northeast and Midwest, the deer tick, *Ixodes dammini*, is the culprit. It ranges from Maine to Florida, and west of the Mississippi. In the South, it's the black-legged tick, *Ixodes scapularis*. (Recent taxonomic research has indicated that these two ticks probably belong to a single species, despite the two names.) In the West, its the *western* black-legged tick, *Ixodes pacificus*, that carries the disease in Nevada, Utah, and the Pacific coast from Northern California to Washington. The western black-legged tick feeds not on deer, but on jackrabbits and lizards. The lone star tick, *Amblyomma americanum*, which also carries Rocky Mountain spotted fever, now carries Lyme disease as well, and ranges through the West and southern Midwest. There is increasing concern that the American dog tick, *Dermacentor variabilis*, may be able to transmit the disease.

Let's take a closer look at the life cycle of one of these, the deer tick, to see how Lyme disease is spread. The tick hatches in the spring, and passes through three stages during its two-year life. In the first, or larval, stage, the immature tick is extremely tiny. It normally attaches itself to the white-footed mouse, its principal host at this stage, and will eat one meal of blood. At this time, it may first pick up the Lyme bacterium from an infected mouse. The tick then molts into the nymph stage, which is about the size of a poppy seed or a pinhead. An infected larva will molt into an infected nymph. The nymphs attach themselves to larger animals, such as dogs, opossums, deer . . . or people. They will eat another blood meal, and may inject some of their own body fluids into the host during the process, thus passing on the Lyme spirochete. The nymph will enlarge in size during its meal, growing as large as a small freckle or mole. After its meal, the tick will drop off into tall grass or bushes, and await its third host, which is usually a deer.

The adult tick is a little larger than the nymph. (See Figure 2, page vi.) It is flat, and about the size of a sesame seed—less than one-tenth of an inch in length—though it becomes larger when engorged with blood. This is the first stage that it is large enough to look like what most people think of as a tick. The adults have eight legs, like a spider, and the male is black, the female dark red and black. When engorged with blood, they turn gray, and may enlarge three to five times in size. The adult tick will eat one last blood meal on a deer, mate, and drop off to lay its eggs. The deer themselves do not always seem to become infected with the Lyme spirochete, but they are an essential host in the tick's life cycle.

The nymphs and the adults are the most likely to infect humans. The nymphs are the biggest threat, because they are hardest to see, and the bites are painless. In fact, it is estimated that 70 to 90 percent of all cases of Lyme disease are caused by nymph bites. The nymphs and adults wait on low vegetation in wooded areas, in neighboring grasslands, or in tall sea grasses by the ocean. They can't fly or jump, but will hitch a ride on whatever warm-blooded animal brushes by. Dogs and other pets can carry the ticks to homes and yards (though it seems that cats are less likely to carry the tick, perhaps because of their constant grooming).

Not all deer ticks actually carry the bacteria that cause Lyme disease, and only an infected tick can transmit Lyme disease. The percentage of infected ticks may vary from only 2 percent in some areas to more than 90 percent in Lyme disease "hot spots." Even an infected tick may not transmit Lyme disease if it is discovered and removed in time. An infected tick must usually feed for 24 to 48 hours before passing the spirochete into the bloodstream of its host, and transmitting the infection.

HOT SPOTS, DANGER ZONES, AND LYME SEASON

Though deer do not actually carry Lyme disease, they do carry the ticks that carry the disease, and the expanding deer population throughout certain regions of the U.S. is a major cause of the spread of Lyme disease. In addition, fewer people are hunting deer for sport, and their natural predators have been disappearing. So deer are not only growing in numbers, but moving into new areas closer to population centers. At the same time, people are moving much closer to deer as suburbs expand into abandoned farmland and houses are scattered through wooded areas.

The real hot spots for Lyme disease are places where suburban lawns meet woodlands, such as Westchester County, just north of New York City, and throughout New Jersey where expanding cities butt up against farmland and woods. The tick population has been exploding along with the deer population; hence the increased rates of infection. In 1982, deer ticks were rare in Westchester County, New York; they now average 1½ ticks per square yard in some study plots. Some of the small East coast islands are also among the hottest spots for Lyme disease. These include popular summer tourist destinations, like Nantucket, Block Island, Fire Island, and even the Florida Keys, where exploding deer populations simply have nowhere to go. There is a high risk of Lyme disease for people who inhabit or visit these areas.

In whatever part of the country, Lyme hot spots are determined by four factors: the number of cases reported; the size of the deer population; the degree of tick infestation; and the percentage of infected ticks. Many state health departments are now keeping epidemiological records on the Lyme risk areas, and can tell you what percentage of ticks are infected in a given locality. Hospitals with Lyme disease clinics may also be able to inform you about local risk areas.

The danger zones are woods, tall grass and brush, marshy areas with tall reeds and grasses, and seashore grassland, but ticks can lurk even in mowed lawns. People who work or pursue hobbies outdoors in the danger zones are at special risk. These include farmers, landscapers, tree surgeons, park rangers, hunters, and hikers. City folk and tourists are at risk as well, from weekend excursions into the country, or serious hiking and camping trips in woods and state parks. Entire families have been infected with Lyme disease, picked up on canoeing or hiking trips.

In the Northwest and Midwest, the months from May through August pose the greatest risk for contracting Lyme disease. This is when the nymphs are active, and most people are out of doors. The rates of infection are somewhat lower on either side of Lyme "season," which includes the months of April, and September through November. The rate is lowest from December through March, but there still is some risk. It is perfectly possible to catch Lyme disease on warm winter days, especially in the endemic areas. People who are out in woods or brush in fall and winter months must still take precautions.

In California, the high-risk season is November to April, and risk seasons may vary in other parts of the country.

PREVENTING LYME DISEASE

By far the best way to deal with Lyme disease at this time is to avoid becoming infected. A Lyme vaccine is currently under study, but at the time of this writing has not yet been proven safe and effective. We do not have an effective means of preventing the spread of the spirochete in the wild, though some local measures have shown promise. Pets and domestic animals are susceptible to Lyme disease, and can increase the risk for humans. Fortunately, there is a vaccine for dogs, but we have to include pets when taking preventive measures. To prevent Lyme disease, we have to begin by guarding against tick bites, and by careful inspection and removal of any ticks that we do pick up.

How to Avoid Tick Bites

First of all, be aware of the high-risk environments for Lyme disease, and the endemic areas and hot spots that you may reside in or travel to. In Lyme disease areas, the high-risk environments include woods and brush, tall grass, marshes, hiking trails, grassy dunes, and the like. The Lyme spirochete loves the seashore just as much as the deep woods. Suburban areas where housing abuts woods or farmland, or anywhere you can see deer, are high-risk areas for Lyme. In state parks or forests, be aware of Lyme warnings. And in Lyme areas, follow these precautions when hiking in the woods, gardening, doing yard work, or walking in tall grass:

- Wear protective clothing. Wear long pants, long-sleeved shirts with button sleeves. Tuck shirts into pants, pants legs into socks, wear closed shoes. Wear light-colored, tightly-woven materials; it's easier to spot ticks on white or tan cloth, and they may not be able to grip to slippery, tight weaves like nylon. In the woods, wear a close-fitting hat or cap; ticks like to get into hair, behind ears.

- Inspect your clothing frequently for ticks while in underbrush or forests. Have a companion inspect your back. Later at home you can do a complete check.
- When hiking, stay in the middle of trails. Don't bushwhack.
- If you are sending your kids to summer camps, make sure the camp has an active tick awareness program. A camp should be showing ticks to counselors, and teaching campers how to dress and check for ticks.
- A judicious use of insect repellent can help protect against ticks. It works best when applied to clothing, rather than bare skin, but is not a substitute for other protective measures.

HOW TO CHECK FOR TICKS

- When you come in from outdoor work or recreation in a high-risk environment, inspect your body carefully for ticks. Especially check the groin, navel, trunk of the body, armpits, head, hairline, and behind knees and ears. Have a companion check your back, or use a mirror.
- Take a shower and shampoo your hair; this may wash off any ticks that are not attached.
- Inspect children at least once daily for ticks, perhaps before bed or at bath time, especially in the summer when they are outdoors. When in heavily infested areas, inspect children every three to four hours. Look in ears, check the navel.
- Remember that the nymph-stage ticks are no bigger than a poppy seed, adults no bigger than a sesame seed. Look for a "a freckle that moves." Or for a mole that you haven't noticed before. A magnifying glass may be helpful if you spot something. Ticks usually crawl for several hours after getting on to a host, so you are likely to catch them before they start to bite.
- After potential exposure, remove clothing, and check for ticks in folds or cuffs. Wash the clothes or put them in a hot dryer for thirty minutes to kill any ticks. Inspect knapsacks, other gear.
- If you have pets or animals that roam outside, you need to check them for ticks as well. Animals can catch Lyme disease.

REMOVING TICKS

If you do find a tick, do not grab it with your fingers and crush it, or twist it off if it's attached. Bacteria from a crushed tick may penetrate even unbroken skin. But the sooner you remove it, the greater your chances of avoiding infection. Remember, ticks must normally feed for at least 24 hours before transmitting an infection.

To remove a crawling tick, you may lightly brush it off with a tissue or handkerchief, or use a piece of sticky tape to pick it up. If the tick is embedded, remove it gently with a pair of fine-tipped tweezers. Apply the tweezers as close to the skin as possible, and tug gently, pulling straight away from the skin. Do not twist as you pull; this could break off the head and mouth parts and leave them embedded in the skin. Avoid squeezing the body of the tick, which could inject bacteria into the skin. Save the tick in a plastic bag or small glass bottle, for later identification. Wipe the skin of the bite with an antiseptic, such as rubbing alcohol, and thoroughly wash hands with soap and water.

Some additional tips:

- Carry "tick tweezers" with you when you garden or hike. You can get these in some sporting goods stores, or just get a pair of fine-tipped tweezers, preferably with curved tips, at your pharmacy.
- If you don't have tweezers or some kind of forceps, put on rubber gloves or cover your fingers with tissue or a paper towel to pull off the tick. And wash your hands later, with alcohol if possible.
- If mouth parts do remain after you remove a tick, use the tweezers to try to remove them, the way you would a splinter. And carefully disinfect the bite with antiseptic.
- Don't squeeze, crush, or puncture the body of the tick. Its saliva or blood or gut contents may contain bacteria. Ticks can carry other infections besides Lyme disease, including Rocky Mountain spotted fever and tularemia.
- Forget about the home remedies for tick removal: gasoline, petroleum jelly, kerosene, fingernail polish, lighted cigarettes, a hot match. These have not been shown to be effective, and may actually increase the risk of infection. Ticks breathe as little as four times an hour, so vaseline won't suffocate them. Hardened nail polish can actually prevent them from leaving. And heat from an extinguished match or a cigarette may cause them to expel infected fluids into the skin.
- If you're in the field, save the tick in a small bottle or plastic bag in case it needs to be identified or inspected later. Put a few blades of grass or a piece of moist paper in the container to keep it from drying out. Later, or at home, put it in a small jar or tightly closed container with rubbing alcohol, and label the container with your

name, address and phone number; the date; the type of host (whether a person or a pet); the body location; and where you think the tick was picked up.

Accurate identification of the tick will become very important if you or a pet develop disease symptoms. Documenting a bite and identifying a tick is especially important if you are in an area where Lyme disease is not considered prevalent, and doctors may not be on the lookout for it. In most areas, you can submit a tick for identification through your local or state health department office. Your doctor or veterinarian may also be able to have a tick identified.

ENVIRONMENTAL MEASURES

There are no effective environmental measures for reducing the risk of Lyme disease, except for small areas. Broad-area spraying of insecticides is not particularly effective, since many ticks are underground in animal burrows or waiting on the underside of leaves where sprays can't reach them. Moreover, insecticides put other insects at risk including beneficial ones, and animals and people as well.

However, there are some things that can be done to reduce tick infestation, at least for backyards and smaller areas. Clearing brush and cutting long grass near homes and buildings will help. So will keeping lawns mowed, and limiting lawn watering. Wood piles attract mice, so these should be moved away from buildings. It's a good idea to move bird feeders to the edge of yards, since birds can carry ticks, and spilled seed attracts other animals.

THE COURSE OF INFECTION

Lyme infection begins with the tick bite, which is not painful in itself, and may not even be noticed. Not every carrier tick is infected with the Lyme spirochete. The rate of infection may be as low as 2 percent in some areas to 90 percent in a Lyme disease hot spot. A bite from a non-infected tick may be seen as a small red spot, after the tick has fallen off or been removed. A skin reaction that takes place within a few hours is probably a reaction to the bite itself, and not to the Lyme spirochete. It is important to note that even an infected tick will not immediately transmit the infection; the tick must be attached for 24 to 48 hours before it is likely to pass on the spirochete.

Once the infection has been transmitted, the symptoms of Lyme disease will vary greatly from person to person. There is no single symptom that occurs in all cases, and no clearly predictable time frame or sequence to the development of symptoms. Still, Lyme disease will progress in three general phases, often with dormant, symptomless periods in between. (It's interesting that syphilis, which is caused by a related spirochete, also progresses through three stages and can also cause multi-system disorders.)

Stage One:
Three to thirty days after a bite by an infected tick, the unique "bull's-eye" rash may appear. The medical term for this is *erythema migrans*, and it appears as a large expanding skin rash around the bite. It can vary in size, shape, and color, but often appears as a red ring with clear center. (It is occasionally bluish, or made up of many separate circles.) Over days, the outer edges may expand from perhaps 2 or 3 inches to as much as 8 or 12 inches in diameter. The rash may have a firm center area, and may feel warm or hot to the touch. The sensation is usually described as burning rather than itching. The rash may grow for several weeks, then fade away. More than one rash may appear, and the rash may disappear briefly and reappear on some other part of the body. It can occur in hard-to-see areas such as the buttocks or scalp. About a third of those bitten by infected ticks may never develop the rash at all. (The absence of the rash is most common in children.)

Along with the rash, or even if no rash is present, an infected person may experience a mild illness with flu-like symptoms, including stiff neck, chills, sore throat, nausea, vomiting, headaches, swollen lymph glands, extreme fatigue, and fever of 100 to 103 degrees Fahrenheit. There may be joint pain during the first weeks, though usually without swelling. There may be "meningitis-like" symptoms of stiff neck and severe headache. One indicator of possible Lyme infection is a "flu" that occurs during summer or early fall, when the ticks are biting, and outside of the normal flu season. Some people do not progress beyond stage one, even if untreated. Nevertheless, if Lyme can be clearly diagnosed at this stage, it is important to treat with antibiotics, to prevent more severe symptoms that may occur many months later.

Stage Two:
This is a transitional stage, extending from about four weeks after infection to several months. In Stage Two, the infection has diffused to various systems of the body, where it presents new symptoms that may shift from one part of the body to another, and may flare up briefly and then disappear. As in Joe's case, these can include muscle aches, extreme fatigue and malaise, and loss of appetite. Sometimes a new set of rashes appears. A common symptom, though it does not occur in all cases, is an arthritis-like pain or swelling of the joints. Usually the knees are affected, but shoulders, elbows or even hands may have symptoms. This is sometimes called "migratory arthritis," because it may move from joint to joint: First one knee is swollen, then an ankle or an elbow. The "Lyme arthritis" may follow a tick bite by many months, and develop in mid-winter or even in spring, long after the usual tick season. Untreated, the arthritis may subside spontaneously, may come and go, or may become chronic. More than half of patients with the skin rash develop arthritis if not treated, but even those who never had the rash can develop major symptoms.

About 20 percent of untreated people develop neurological or cardiac disorders. The spirochete doesn't like to remain in the bloodstream, but burrows into tissue and even into the cerebrospinal fluid, where it can infect the nerves and brain. Infection of the heart's nerves and electrical system can cause various symptoms, including a slowing heart rate, pain near the heart, shortness of breath, palpitations and irregular heart rhythms, or arrhythmias. About 5 percent of those infected develop cardiac problems, and may even require a temporary pacemaker. These are difficult cases, since doctors may not suspect Lyme disease as the cause of heart problems.

Neurological symptoms can include impaired motor coordination, dizziness, and severe headaches that resemble viral meningitis. Also common is a type of facial paralysis called Bell's palsy that makes one side of the face droop. Bell's palsy is the most typical neurological complication. It is caused by inflammation of the nerves that control the muscles on one side of the face. Other nerves may become inflamed, causing pain or weakness in the shoulders and upper arms. Optic nerves may be affected, causing symptoms of conjunctivitis. The spirochete may infect the lining of the brain (meningitis), or the brain itself (encephalitis), causing a whole range of symptoms, including depression, poor concentration, mental confusion, memory loss, and movement disorders, even temporary paralysis.

The severity of Second Stage symptoms varies greatly from

individual to individual, but they can often be quite debilitating. Very often, symptoms may disappear within a few weeks, only to return after another dormant period. Or a different body system may be affected. Lyme disease is still treatable at this point, usually with oral antibiotics, though it requires a much longer course of antibiotic treatment than many other infections. The Lyme spirochete is still "exploring" the body, and has not yet settled in and become a chronic infection.

Stage Three:

If untreated, or treated inadequately, Lyme disease may persist and cause chronic symptoms beginning many months after infection, and lasting for years. In Stage Three, symptoms become persistent, or recur with great regularity. About 50 percent of untreated people develop recurring or chronic arthritis after a latent period of up to two years. (The disease was first called Lyme arthritis.) The arthritis almost always affects the knees, and can make walking difficult. (Long Island residents called it "Montauk knee.") Stage Three Lyme disease can sometimes result in permanent structural damage to the joints. Studies show that late-stage Lyme arthritis is mediated by the immune system, and sometimes looks like rheumatoid arthritis, as it did in the first cases reported in Lyme, Connecticut. There is sometimes chronic skin disease, especially a rash of the extremities, the hands and feet, though this is seen more in Europe than in the U.S.

Stage Three also may be marked by severe neurological symptoms, including profound fatigue and malaise, confusion, disturbance of vision, depression, memory loss, numbness and tingling that resembles multiple sclerosis, facial paralysis, and even seizures. Some confused and forgetful sufferers of Lyme disease have been misdiagnosed as having Alzheimer's disease.

At this chronic stage, Lyme disease requires extended treatment with antibiotics, which may be administered intravenously or through intramuscular injection. Relapses may occur, even after extended antibiotic treatment. Some researchers speculate that the spirochete may induce an immune system disorder, or an autoimmune reaction, that can persist in the form of arthritis even after the infection has been eradicated. Neurological symptoms are often the most persistent, and resistant to treatment, because it is hard for antibiotics and the immune system to cross the blood/brain barrier that separates the bloodstream from the cerebrospinal fluid.

It is important to note that with Lyme disease, these stages are not cut in stone. An infected person doesn't always start in Stage One with all the classic symptoms, and move step-by-step through Stage

Two and Stage Three. Very often symptoms overlap between the stages. Symptoms vary greatly from individual to individual. An infected person may go for many months without symptoms, and then suddenly fall into Stage Three Lyme disease, with severe, multisystem complications. The classic symptoms, such as the rash, and swollen, painful joints, may not always appear. Extreme fatigue is one symptom that does seem to persist through all three stages, but this may be misdiagnosed as a symptom of other diseases, or as psychosomatic in nature. It may be interpreted as chronic fatigue syndrome, by patients or by doctors. For all of these reasons, and because the initial tick bite is so often overlooked, correct diagnosis of Lyme disease can be a real challenge to the physician. Let's take a look at the steps a doctor will go through in making a diagnosis.

DIAGNOSIS: THE STANDARD PROCEDURE

There are many significant indicators for Lyme disease that can make a typical diagnosis easy. We would look for a tick bite, the bull's-eye rash, and flu-like symptoms followed by Bell's palsy, an abnormal electrocardiogram, swollen or painful joints, and a positive result on the blood antibody test. In typical cases, like that of my young patient Joe, the diagnosis is pretty easy to make, and the improvement with treatment and the follow-up blood test confirm the diagnosis. Unfortunately, Lyme disease shows up very differently in different individuals, does not always show a positive blood test, and may resist treatment in advanced stages. Symptoms may come and go, and may shift from one body system to another. We call it "the Great Imitator," because it can mimic so many other diseases, from rheumatoid arthritis to multiple sclerosis to chronic fatigue syndrome.

Still, we can follow a standard procedure in making a diagnosis, weighing three different factors: a detailed case history; epidemiological evidence (the likelihood of exposure); and last, and probably least significant, the tests of blood and other fluids.

Of these, the medical history is probably most important, and should be supported by a thorough physical exam. This may take some time, since the doctor should conduct a range of tests to rule out other diseases. A patient may come to a doctor convinced she has Lyme disease or chronic fatigue syndrome, but both patient and doctor must keep an open mind, and carefully think through both the possibility of Lyme disease and the possibility of other illness. The rash is a good indicator, but many people do not connect the appearance of a rash to a tick bite that might have occurred weeks earlier. There can be great variation in the appearance of Lyme rash that may confuse diagnosis. Though it often looks like the classic red ring around a light-colored center, it can vary from a reddish blotchy appearance to red throughout. And it can be confused with poison ivy, a spider or insect bite, or ringworm. If you have an unusual rash and suspect Lyme disease, try to document it by taking a picture, because it could disappear before a physician can see it. A picture could be worth 10,000 words! Remember, though, a significant percentage of patients don't have the rash at all, especially children. The point is, we can't focus too much on this in making a diagnosis. The flu-like symptoms are also a helpful indicator, especially if they follow appearance of a rash. The next set of indicators usually come with Stage Two Lyme disease, as previously described. See page 26 for a symptom checklist.

If someone comes into my office complaining of body aches and fatigue, or a whole range of diffuse symptoms that haven't been clearly diagnosed or effectively treated, I first do a whole battery of routine tests, including blood tests and urinalysis. I test the white blood cell count, and test for liver disease (including hepatitis), kidney disease, muscle disease, specific infections, and autoimmune disease, including lupus and rheumatoid arthritis. If there's a possibility of Lyme infection, I'll do an electrocardiogram, which could reveal arrhythmia caused by Lyme disease. I test for vitamin B_{12} levels in the blood, because even borderline B_{12} deficiency can cause fatigue and neurological symptoms. I test for thyroid disease, which can cause muscle aches and fatigue. I'll check for *Candida* (yeast) infection, which can cause extreme fatigue similar to that of Lyme disease. And in some cases I'll call for an MRI image of the brain, to rule out possible structural damage caused by multiple sclerosis or a tumor. Some of these tests are pretty standard; others I'll apply depending on the patient's specific symptoms. In some cases, an antibody test for Lyme disease is clearly called for, though we can't lean too heavily on the results, as we'll see below.

DIAGNOSTIC CHECK LIST FOR LYME DISEASE

Please note: having a number of these symptoms does not *in itself* constitute a diagnosis of Lyme disease. This list is to assist you and your physician in building up a diagnostic picture. A final diagnosis must be made by an experienced doctor.

EARLY SYMPTOMS
- Tick bite _____
- Rash at the bite site _____
- Expanding rash or multiple rashes _____
- Flu-like symptoms in summer or early fall _____
- Unexplained fevers, sweats, chills, flushing _____
- Severe headache _____
- Sore throat _____
- Swollen glands _____
- Sore or swollen joints _____
- Sore or swollen jaw joint _____
- Stiffness of joints, neck, back _____
- Severe fatigue _____

LATER SYMPTOMS
- Facial paralysis, either side (Bell's Palsy) _____
- Blurry vision, floaters _____
- Arthritis-like joint pain or swelling, especially in knees _____
- Joint pain "migrates" to different joints _____
- Achy, painful muscles _____
- Loss of appetite, unexplained weight loss _____
- Persistent headache _____
- Chest pain, heart palpitations, shortness of breath _____
- Confusion, difficulty thinking or concentrating _____
- Forgetfulness, poor short-term memory _____
- Dizziness, light-headedness, difficulty walking _____
- Mood swings, irritability, depression _____
- Profound fatigue and malaise _____

The second major factor to consider is the epidemiological evidence. Does the patient live or work in a known Lyme hot spot? Did the symptoms develop weeks or months after a camping trip, or a vacation by the sea in one of the high Lyme areas? I take a travel history, and try to rule out parasites, or exotic tropical infectious diseases. If a patient comes in who works as a landscaper on Long Island, or a park ranger in New Jersey, I give that considerable weight, even if their symptoms have developed outside of the normal Lyme season.

The final factors to be considered are the results of antibody tests and other tests for Lyme disease. And these really come last in importance, since the test results are not conclusive. A positive result may confirm a diagnosis of Lyme disease, but a negative test does not rule one out. Let's take a closer look at the most common tests, and some recently developed and rarely used ones as well.

TESTING FOR LYME DISEASE

It is difficult, though possible, to test for the actual Lyme spirochete in an infected person. The spirochete that causes Lyme disease can indeed be cultured from a biopsy, or small bit of skin, taken from the Lyme rash. This is a difficult and expensive process, however, and it's still possible to miss seeing the spirochete under the microscope. Besides, not every infected person has the rash. Since the spirochete doesn't linger in the bloodstream but burrows quickly into tissue or cerebrospinal fluid, sometimes within a few hours, it's not possible to directly detect it in the bloodstream.

What we can detect, in some cases, are antibodies that the immune system produces in response to the infection. (Antibodies are special proteins that the body produces to attack invading bacteria, or neutralize the toxins they produce.) The Lyme spirochete can induce a characteristic mix of antibodies, which can be identified through a test of a blood sample taken from an infected person. This standard antibody test is called the ELISA test, for "Enzyme-Linked Immunosorbent Assay." This is in fact the same technique that is used to test for the AIDS virus, which shows a different pattern of antibodies. A lab in an endemic area may conduct more than a thousand ELISA tests a week during the height of Lyme season.

There are several problems with the ELISA test, which make its results less than conclusive. First, it takes time for the Lyme spirochete to activate the immune system to produce the antibodies, so tests will show up as negative for the first four to six weeks after a tick-induced infection. Thus an infected person will most likely test negative for Lyme disease throughout the entire First Stage. During this period, Lyme can only be diagnosed by evidence of a tick bite, presence of a rash, and medical history. If the medical history indicates possible Lyme disease, an initial negative test result should always be followed up four to six weeks later.

Second, the immune system often mounts a very weak response to Lyme infection, especially in older persons, making it harder to detect antibodies at any stage of the disease.

Third, early treatment with antibiotics, even if they have not eradicated the infection, will tend to make the ELISA test results show up as negative, even where there is chronic late stage Lyme disease. People who have been treated with low doses or short courses of antibiotics, for whatever reason, simply cannot get a reliable indication from the antibody test. They can wind up with advanced, chronic Lyme disease that is easily confused with arthritis, chronic fatigue syndrome, and so on, while getting consistently negative results from the antibody test.

It's even possible for someone with syphilis to show up as positive on a Lyme test, since the syphilis spirochete induces a similar antibody response. In fact, there is a whole array of conditions that can cause false positive results on the ELISA test, including syphilis, leptospirosis (caused by another spirochete), relapsing fever, HIV infection, infectious mononucleosis, Rocky Mountain spotted fever, rheumatoid arthritis, and lupus erythematosis. All of these must be ruled out before a positive Lyme result is indicated.

Nevertheless, the test does have some diagnostic benefits. If Lyme infection goes untreated, the ELISA test usually shows up as positive a few weeks after exposure. It is virtually always positive in untreated patients with Lyme arthritis.

A second, backup, antibody test is the Western blot. This again looks for a pattern of antibodies as they migrate across a piece of blotter paper in an electric field. It is a more sensitive test that can be used to confirm a positive ELISA test. The downside? Interpretation of the Western blot depends to some extent on the skill, experience, and subjective judgment of the clinician who is reviewing the results. It's a little like reading tea leaves and looking for a pattern. It does not present an open-and-shut case.

Individual labs and doctors have experimented with other kinds of tests. One measures the response of white blood cells called T cells to the presence of the spirochete in a test tube. An active response may indicate that the patient has been exposed to Lyme. Some have looked for evidence of the spirochete in urine. Others have used a spinal tap to observe fragments of the spirochete in cerebrospinal fluid, or even to culture live bacteria from this source. Most of these tests are experimental; none are in wide use.

There is one recent development, however, that shows real promise as a test for Lyme disease. This is called the PCR test, for "Polymerase Chain Reaction." The PCR test can detect an extremely small quantity of genetic material from the Lyme spirochete, on the order of 10 individual bacteria in a milliliter of fluid, and "amplify" it so that it can be detected. So far, studies have used PCR to detect the spirochete in samples of blood serum, urine, cerebrospinal fluid and synovial fluid (which lubricates joints like the knee joint). This test is highly specific to the Lyme spirochete, with a very low percentage of false positive results. Though still under study, the PCR test may be extremely useful for confirming a diagnosis of Lyme disease, and also may help us track the movement and life cycle of the spirochete within the body. The PCR test has already been able to identify the spirochete or fragments of it in some people who were told they did not have Lyme, or who had not been successfully treated.

Unfortunately, as with the antibody tests, PCR gives negative or indefinite results in about half of patients who seem to have very definite or probable advanced Lyme disease. This may mean that the spirochete has actually disappeared, or persists in numbers too low to be tested, even by PCR. The possibility exists that advanced Lyme may cause arthritic or neurological damage, or immune system imbalance, · that persists even after the Lyme spirochete has been eradicated. So like the other tests, PCR can support a diagnosis, but cannot by itself rule out the possibility of Lyme disease.[1] With future refinement, however, it may better guide the decision of whether to continue antibiotic treatment.

WHEN IS TREATMENT RECOMMENDED?

If you have a clear diagnosis of Lyme disease, based on a bite from a tick known to be infected, on the typical rash, on a positive blood test, and on typical symptoms, antibiotic treatment should begin without delay. However, as we've noted, a clear-cut Lyme diagnosis is not always possible, especially in the first stage of the disease. Suppose you've been in an endemic area, received some kind of unusual insect bite, and feel a little "off" a few days later. But you found no tick, have no indicator rash, and can't decide if you really feel something like the flu or just a passing headache or indigestion. Or suppose you find a tick. What then? Do you rush to your doctor and demand antibiotic treatment, or wait it out to see if the bite clears up and if you feel better in a couple of days? Some anxiety about Lyme would be normal, given the seriousness of the complications and the alarming stories in the press. But opinions differ on the wisdom of "prophylactic" treatment with antibiotics to prevent progression of a possible infection.

If you've had a tick bite, for example, but no other symptoms, this is not an entirely comfortable situation. But in general I would say it does no harm to sit tight for a few days or a week. Check your temperature and record it, jot down any symptoms you might have, note any changes in the insect bite. If you have any kind of rash or unusual bite, take a photograph of it for later reference. If you did find a tick, remove it carefully and save it in a glass bottle. (See pages 10–20 on how to remove a tick safely.)

Check in with your doctor by phone, if you like, just to let her or him know about your concerns. Remember, even a bite from an infected tick will not pass the infection unless it has been feeding for 24 to 48 hours. Starting a long course of high-dosage antibiotics is not an inconsequential decision. There are risks of side effects, and this kind of treatment puts its own real stress on your system. On the other hand, if some kind of rash develops, or you run a fever or develop severe headaches or fatigue, go ahead and see your doctor. It's time for a medical opinion. In any case, keep your notes for the record. If new symptoms appear weeks or a month or two later, you'll be much more likely to get a definitive ELISA test with a clear diagnosis, and treatment at this stage is still effective.

There is one condition in which you'd probably want to get a medical opinion right away, and consider treatment sooner rather than later, and that is if you're pregnant. Pregnant women are at particular risk, and there have been reports of miscarriages, premature births, stillbirths, birth defects, and of the passing on of Lyme disease to the fetus. There have been no reports of infection transferred through breast feeding.

TREATING LYME DISEASE: STAGES ONE AND TWO

The standard treatment for Lyme disease, at any stage, is antibiotic therapy. To this, I think it's important to add a holistic component, to prevent or compensate for the unwanted effects of antibiotic treatment, and to restore the whole body to health. Proper diet, lifestyle changes, and certain vitamins and nutrients can make a great contribution in treating Lyme disease, especially after a long and debilitating course of illness. When Lyme is diagnosed and treated early, or even in the Second Stage, it can be effectively cured with oral antibiotics, with no further symptoms. However, there have been few thorough studies of how to treat Lyme, even in early stages, so most of our knowledge is based on trial and error. The field is still evolving, and even now there are no generally accepted protocols for treating Lyme, though we have learned much about what works and what doesn't. We have learned that some antibiotics are more effective than others in preventing relapses and progression of the disease. We have learned that longer courses of treatment are needed for Lyme than for many other bacterial infections. If you have been diagnosed with Lyme disease, it's important that your doctor keep up with the current information about effective treatment.

Soon after infection, the Lyme spirochete rapidly migrates to all parts of the body, including the central nervous system. So even in the earliest stages, antibiotics must be used that have the ability to penetrate all body tissues. And they must be given in higher dosage than for other kinds of infections, because they have to be able to penetrate deep into tissue and cross the blood/brain barrier. There is no one universally effective antibiotic. As of this writing, certain antibiotics of the tetracycline family, such as doxycycline and minocycline, are often used to treat early Lyme disease. Different antibiotics, especially those of the penicillin family, like amoxicillin, may be used for children and pregnant or lactating women.[2]

Besides the right choice and dosage of antibiotics, it's especially important that the treatment continue long enough to completely eradicate the spirochete, or relapses may occur, and become increasingly harder to treat. It seems that the Lyme spirochete can "lie low" in the body for long periods of time, so it's important to continue treatment well beyond its dormant, or generative, period. Up to the mid-1980s, many Lyme patients were treated with short courses of antibiotics, lasting seven to ten days. Relapses and recurring symptoms were common, and a number of patients progressed to late stage Lyme, which is harder to treat. Some Lyme patients received short-course antibiotic treatment for their symptoms, but without a clear diagnosis of Lyme disease. Not only did this complicate later treatment, but it tended to make ELISA tests come up negative, complicating later diagnosis as well.[3]

Many Lyme specialists now believe that even early treatment should last for four to six weeks, or should continue at least four weeks beyond the disappearance of all symptoms. Stage Two Lyme might be treated for at least six weeks, and then six weeks beyond the disappearance of all symptoms. Because the course of Lyme disease can vary greatly from person to person, both the choice of antibiotic and the duration of treatment should be tailored to the individual patient. Symptoms may not clear up right away, but may start to gradually improve after weeks of treatment, or even after treatment has ended. If symptoms recur, it's important to relate this information to your doctor.[4]

RISKS OF ANTIBIOTIC TREATMENT

This kind of extended course of antibiotics is not without its own health risks. Besides encouraging the growth of resistant strains of harmful bacteria, sustained, high-dosage antibiotics have a drastic effect on the body's own natural "ecology." They tend to kill off beneficial bacteria that line the intestinal tract, and aid in digestion. In their absence, other harmful bacteria may take hold. The yeast organism called Candida is especially likely to proliferate in the denuded intestinal tract, causing serious illness of its own. For these reasons, I think it's important to supplement the body's own defenses and natural ecology with essential nutrients, and to replenish the devastated digestive bacteria with acidophilus from unsweetened yogurt or powder.

There are other potential risks to antibiotic treatment that range in effect from the merely annoying to the actually life-threatening. Anyone who is considering a long-term course of antibiotics, or who has undergone several repeated courses, should be aware of these. Symptoms can include: skin rash; hearing changes; a mottled appearance of the tongue; taste disturbances; a metallic taste in mouth; appetite suppression; nausea or cramps; ulceration; diarrhea or alternately constipation due to deletion of intestinal flora; vaginitis in women; rectal problems including rashes, itching, fissures, exacerbated hemorrhoids; and spaciness or malaise.

Doxycycline, which is commonly used to treat Lyme, can cause increased sun sensitivity, and anyone under this kind of treatment should stay out of the sun and cover up when out of doors. When treating Lyme disease, there is often a flare-up of symptoms a few days or a week after the beginning of antibiotic treatment. The patient may actually feel much worse for a few days, but this is usually a temporary effect.

Some patients are allergic to various antibiotics, especially those of the penicillin family, and the synthetic cephalosporins, like ceftriaxone, which are commonly used in treating advanced Lyme. Allergic reactions can include rashes and flushing, but also life-threatening reactions like anaphylactic shock, which is marked by rapid onset of flushing, and the swelling up of throat and larynx, even to the point of suffocation. Ceftriaxone can also cause gall bladder disturbances, even to the point of requiring surgery to remove the organ. Women and children seem to be at greater risk of developing gall bladder problems.

Advanced Lyme disease (Stage Three) is often treated with extended intravenous antibiotic treatment. This may require the use of "in-dwelling" catheters, IV needles that are placed in the chest wall or in a peripheral vein like in the biceps, to feed the antibiotics into a large vein leading directly to the heart. If not carefully monitored, the catheter can provide a pathway for organisms to infect the bloodstream directly. Serious blood-borne infections may then require additional antibiotics for treatment, further disrupting the body's natural "ecology."

For all these reasons, antibiotic therapy is not to be undertaken lightly. It must be based on a careful diagnosis, and supported by holistic health measures. Although antibiotic therapy does provide a powerful tool for successful treatment of Lyme disease, it must be seen as only one component of a general plan of treatment, along with a healthy diet, nutrient supplements, immune support, physical rehabilitation, and treatment of any lingering damage to joints and nervous system.

ADVANCED LYME DISEASE

Diagnosing advanced Lyme disease can be a real challenge for even the most highly skilled and experienced doctor. Lyme disease can effectively mimic a whole range of other diseases, from multiple sclerosis to chronic fatigue syndrome to autoimmune disease. And it's entirely possible that a patient may really have an additional chronic illness, such as osteoarthritis or *Candida* infection, that can complicate diagnosis further, and persist after Lyme has been treated. As we've mentioned, early treatment of any kind with antibiotics can cause later negative results from Lyme tests, even in well-established disease. Sometimes a doctor will do a spinal tap to try to identify the spirochete in cerebrospinal fluid, but results are not always conclusive. What's worse, Lyme becomes increasingly resistant to treatment the longer it has been left untreated, or treated inadequately. And there are some patients who never seem to get rid of all their symptoms with the currently available treatments, so we can't even use response to treatment to confirm a supposition of Lyme disease.

TREATING ADVANCED LYME DISEASE

Antibiotics are only one dimension of the treatment of late stage Lyme disease. If we are going to use long courses of powerful antibiotics, we have to support patients' health with vitamins, nutrients, and other natural means to ward off some of the dangerous side effects of the antibiotics. In most cases, we should also use vitamins and nutrients to treat the lingering effects of the illness. These include symptoms of arthritis and immune disorders that can persist even after the spirochete has been eradicated—the so-called "post-Lyme syndrome." We must also use physical therapy to rehabilitate patients who have been exhausted and sometimes bedridden, and have experienced the wasting of unused muscles and the stiffening of painful joints. There are psychological dimensions to consider as well, and some promising alternative treatments. Let's take a closer look at these different approaches.

ANTIBIOTICS

Despite the high cost and serious side effects, antibiotic treatment remains a powerful and effective tool that can return wasted, debilitated victims of chronic Lyme disease to some semblance of normal, pain-free life. The challenge for antibiotic therapy is to somehow get the drugs across the blood/brain barrier, and deep into the body tissue, the cerebrospinal fluid, and the synovial fluid of joints where the Lyme spirochete has secreted itself. To do this, doctors may use a combination of drugs, like amoxicillin and probenecid, or one of the new synthetic antibiotics, like ceftriaxone. An intravenous drip or an infusion pump may be needed to keep a sufficient or accurately-measured quantity of the antibiotic constantly in the system.

There are side effects to extended, high-dose antibiotic therapy, some of them merely uncomfortable, some serious. Many patients experience an exacerbation of symptoms at some point during treatment, such as increased muscle pain, increased fatigue, nausea, and malaise. These are probably caused by the die-off of the spirochete and an immune reaction to the release of dead organisms into tissue and bloodstream. In some cases, especially in children, certain antibiotics like Rocephin can damage the gall bladder. Unless properly cared for, an IV needle can be a point of entry for infection. And antibiotics definitely disturb the ecology of the body, especially the intestinal tract. If not properly managed, antibiotic treatment can induce vaginitis, gastrointestinal problems, and secondary infections with *Candida* yeast. It can even cause pseudomembranous colitis, an overgrowth of bacteria related to the one that causes botulism.

This is why we can't simply administer antibiotics and leave it at that. Rather, we have to treat Lyme patients in a more holistic way, supporting them against the stress of antibiotics, treating the lingering effects of Lyme disease, including the immune-mediated consequences. This can be especially important for older patients who are experiencing the natural decline of immune function with age. Let's look at a standard protocol for the holistic treatment of advanced Lyme disease.

A HEALTHY DIET FOR RECOVERY

The ideal diet for aiding recovery from Lyme disease offers other healthful benefits as well. It will reduce the likelihood of yeast infection. It will alter the balance of prostaglandin hormones in the body to reduce inflammation. It will promote cardiovascular health, prevent weight gain, and guard against diabetes and degenerative disease. What is this miracle diet? Here's the simple outline:

- Avoid sugar, including "natural sugars" in fruit juice, maple syrup, honey, dried fruit, and the like. Avoid refined carbohydrates and starchy vegetables that are too quickly converted into glucose in the bloodstream.
- To guard against yeast infection, avoid yeast-containing foods like bread, baked goods, cheese, mushrooms, vinegar, soy sauce, fermented foods like pickles and olives, and beer and alcohol. Alcohol is a significant factor in failed antibiotic treatment.
- Do eat plentiful amounts of cruciferous vegetables such as broccoli, cauliflower and cabbage, and dark green leafy vegetables.
- If there are symptoms of arthritis, avoid the nightshade family of vegetables (tomatoes, eggplant, green peppers and potatoes) which can promote arthritis.
- Do eat whole grains which convert more slowly into blood sugar.
- Do eat beans, lentils, and other legumes.
- Do eat protein in the form of tofu or lean meat.
- Do eat foods rich in omega-3 essential oils, such as fish, walnuts and flax seed. These beneficial oils affect the prostaglandin balance in the body, and reduce inflammation.
- Avoid saturated fats, margarine, and butter; use more monounsaturated olive oil.
- Do eat foods that are nutrient rich but not calorie dense, since Lyme disease sufferers usually cannot exercise and are susceptible to weight gain which further weakens the body and degrades health.

NUTRIENTS AND VITAMINS TO SUPPORT HEALTH

Nutrient and vitamin supplements can be used to support the healing process, to protect against the effects of antibiotic treatment, and to combat the lingering effects of post-Lyme syndrome. Here follows a complete protocol. Some of these nutrients will be useful for nearly all Lyme patients, even during treatment of Stage One and Stage Two Lyme disease. Others may be effective for treating advanced Lyme disease, and for specific lingering symptoms. It's important to note that therapy with vitamins and nutrients is generally effective on a long-term, slow-acting basis. In many cases, therapy must be applied for three to four months before symptoms will begin to improve.

First of all, there are some things we can do to maintain the beneficial bacteria, the "flora," of the intestinal tract. The following natural remedies, available in most health foods stores, can be especially helpful:

- *Acidophilus.* This is a natural culture of beneficial bacteria that can be used to help maintain the proper "ecological balance" in the digestive tract. Many brands of yogurt have active acidophilus cultures, so one way to keep up the balance is to eat a cup of this type of unsweetened yogurt every day. Those who don't like yogurt or may be allergic to milk products can take acidophilus in the form of powder or capsules. **Recommended dosage:** Powder—¼ to ½ teaspoon 3 times daily. Capsules—2 capsules 3 times daily.
- *Fructose oligosaccharides (FOS).* This is a good food source for beneficial bacteria, which does not fuel the growth of yeast (*Candida*). **Recommended dosage:** ½ teaspoon 3 times daily. There are also several natural inhibitors of yeast growth, which can be used during antibiotic treatment. By using these, you can avoid the risk of drug interactions between antibiotics and prescription anti-yeast drugs like nystatin.
- *Garlic.* To avoid problems of breath and taste, take 2 capsules of garlic concentrate 2 to 3 times daily.
- *Caprylic acid.* **Recommended dosage:** one 300 mg tablet 1 to 2 times daily, with food.
- *Grapefruit seed extract.* Sometimes sold as *Paramicrocidin* or other brand names. **Recommended dosage:** 2 capsules 3 to 4 times daily.

Second, we can use a number of vitamins, minerals and nutrients to support healing, restore balance to the immune system, and treat arthritis at the same time. First among these are the antioxidants and the antioxidant precursors and cofactors. Whenever there is an inflammatory reaction in the body, toxic substances called free radicals are released. These free radicals can cause further damage to tissue, which again increases the inflammation in a kind of vicious circle. Lyme disease often causes inflammation, whether of the joints (arthritis), of the muscles (fibromyalgia), or of the brain or nervous system (encephalitis, meningitis, neuralgia). Enhancing the antioxidant reaction in the body can help relieve symptoms that linger even when the spirochete is dormant or conquered.

- *Vitamin C.* This is an essential antioxidant, which can support healing before, during, and after antibiotic treatment. Vitamin C can also stimulate immune cells to attack *Candida* and harmful bacteria. Ester-C and buffered C are both more easily tolerated in the gastrointestinal tract. **Recommended dosage:** Ester-C—550 mg tablets, 6 or 8 a day. Buffered C—1000 mg tablets, 6 to 8 a day.

  High doses of vitamin C sometimes induce side effects, including diarrhea, gas and bloating, which can compound the side effects of the antibiotics themselves. In this case, lower the oral dosage of vitamin C to 1000 mg or 2000 mg a day. I sometimes provide an intravenous drip of vitamin C in my office, which is more easily tolerated in higher doses during antibiotic treatment. When IV antibiotics are used, it's best to use the lower oral dose, though some innovative home care companies will agree to administer IV vitamins during antibiotic treatment.
- *Bioflavonoids* are often utilized as companion nutrients with vitamin C. They have an antioxidant effect, and also diminish capillary permeability, which may reduce some of the joint inflammation associated with Lyme disease.
- *Vitamin E* has both an anti-inflammatory and immune regulating effect. **Recommended dosage:** up to 800 I.U. a day.
- *Zinc, copper and manganese* are co-factors for the activity of superoxide dismutase (SOD), which is one of the body's own naturally-produced anti-inflammatory enzymes. (It is not effective to give SOD itself orally or by injection.) **Recommended dosage:** copper—2 mg twice daily: zinc—30 mg twice daily; manganese—50 mg twice daily. Zinc and manganese also function directly as antioxidants. Be aware that excess zinc can create copper deficiency and depress immune function, so it's important not to consume more than 90 mg per day.
- *N-acetyl-cysteine* is an amino acid and *selenium* is a mineral; together they function as precursors for glutathione peroxidase, another of the body's own natural antioxidants. **Recommended dosage:** N-acetyl-cysteine—600 mg capsule three times daily. Selenium—200 mcg tablet twice daily.
- *Beta-carotene* is an important antioxidant from which the body can also synthesize vitamin A, an important infection-fighting nutrient, which is also essential for tissue repair. **Recommended dosage:** 25,000 I.U. daily.
- *Vitamin A* has no antioxidant effects, but seems to be an immune-regulator that helps fight infection, and also assists with cellular repair and regeneration. Studies have shown that it increases the resistance of malnourished children to viral diseases. **Recommended dosage:** 10,000 I.U. daily, or up to 50,000 under a doctor's supervision.

Many health food stores offer special antioxidant tablets or capsules that combine all of the above factors. It may be necessary to boost these with additional vitamin C and vitamin E.

The B vitamins play a key role in cellular metabolism, energy production, and cellular growth and repair. They can be especially helpful in repairing neurological damage and supporting energy pathways for those suffering from profound fatigue. A good B-complex is, therefore, a good starting point for Lyme sufferers. B vitamins must be taken "in balance," since an excess of one may cause a deficiency of another. Accordingly, it's wise to follow the recommendations of a nutritionally-oriented physician. The following B vitamins may be considered:

- *Vitamin B$_1$* is associated with energy production and stability of the autonomic nervous system. Vitamin B$_1$ "primes the pump" of the carbohydrate-metabolism pathway, and facilitates the turning of carbohydrates into energy. It may be helpful to the many Lyme patients who become weak and debilitated, and suffer from symptoms of faintness, wooziness, dizziness, palpitations. **Recommended dosage:** 100 mg twice daily.
- *Vitamin B$_2$* is essentially an antioxidant, and can work in cooperation with the other antioxidant vitamins. **Recommended dosage:** 50 mg twice daily.
- *Vitamin B$_3$* deficiencies are associated with dementia and loss of cognitive abilities. Niacinamide is the safer form of supplementation, and may help chronic Lyme sufferers with neurological symptoms. It also has been used to treat symptoms of osteoarthritis. **Recommended dosage:** 100 mg twice daily, or higher under supervision of a nutritionally oriented physician to monitor for liver toxicity.
- *Vitamin B$_6$* has been shown to reduce neurological pain. **Recommended dosage:** 50 to 200 mg daily. Warning: higher doses may cause toxic neurological side effects.
- *Vitamin B$_{12}$* is effective in raising energy levels and in treating fatigue and malaise. **Recommended oral dosage:** 500 to 1,000 mcg daily, especially in sublingual form. Vitamin B$_{12}$ injections are also effective.
- *Inositol* is a constituent of the myelin sheath that surrounds the nerves, and may assist in the repair of neurological damage. **Recommended dosage** for nerve repair: 500 to 1,000 mg 2 to 3 times daily.

Other nutrients may be specifically helpful in treating the profound fatigue of Lyme disease, which may have a metabolic origin.

- *Magnesium* plays an important role in restoring cellular metabolism and replenishing depleted energy reserves. It acts as a catalyst for many of the body's energy reactions. It turns out that many people who suffer from chronic fatigue syndrome are magnesium-deficient. Documented studies have shown these patients to respond to magnesium injections with increased energy. **Recommended oral dosage:** magnesium oxide or magnesium citrate—150 to 200 mg 2 to 3 times daily. Diarrhea is a possible side effect. Some physicians favor the use of magnesium malate because of reputed benefits in treating fibromyalgia.
- *L-carnitine* is an amino acid that acts as a shuttle for fat that is required for cellular metabolism. It can be used as a "cellular energizer" for those suffering from the fatigue of chronic Lyme disease or post-Lyme syndrome. It also acts to strengthen the heart, in case of cardiac symptoms. **Recommended dosage:** 500 to 1,000 mg 2 to 3 times daily.
- *N-acetyl-carnitine* is a related nutrient that in some studies has shown promise in the treatment of chronic fatigue syndrome. Some researchers suggest that this form is more bio-available. **Recommended dosage:** 120 mg 3 times daily. Should be taken between meals, since amino acids are best absorbed on an empty stomach.
- *Coenzyme Q-10* is an essential coenzyme for energy production within the mitochondria, which are the "powerhouses" of cells, and may prove helpful for patients suffering from profound fatigue. Coenzyme Q-10 is also specifically helpful for patients suffering from a weakening of the heart. **Recommended dosage:** 30 mg twice daily.

EFAS

Another set of nutrients may be helpful in treating the arthritis and joint pain of advanced Lyme disease and the auto-immune aspects of post-Lyme syndrome. These include the essential fatty acids—the omega-6 and omega-3 oils. These have been shown to help in treating arthritis, and particularly rheumatoid arthritis, which is immune-mediated, as Lyme arthritis may be. Both omega-6 and omega-3 oils work together through different pathways to reduce the inflammatory prostaglandins associated with the immune response. Both work against inflammation, and against an over-active immune response, and may, therefore, be useful in treating post-Lyme syndrome.

- *Borage oil* is a source of gamma linolenic acid (GLA), an omega-6 oil. It has been shown to improve symptoms of rheumatoid arthritis as well as multiple sclerosis, an auto-immune disease of the central nervous system. **Recommended dosage:** 6 240 mg capsules a day. It may be necessary to build up the dosage gradually to establish tolerance. GLA can be used before, during and after antibiotic treatment.

- *Fish Oil* is a source of eicosopentenoic acid (EPA), an omega-3 oil, which has similar effects to GLA, through a related but different metabolic pathway. **Recommended dosage:** 2 to 3 1000- to 1200-mg capsules three times daily.
- *Shark cartilage* and *bovine cartilage* have both been used to treat arthritis, and new studies suggest that "antigen-feeding" of cartilage may interrupt the autoimmune process in diseases like rheumatoid arthritis. Some physicians treating Lyme disease have recommended these. **Recommended dosage** of shark cartilage: 6 to 9 750- to 1,000-mg capsules daily.
- *Extract of bovine myelin* has been shown to attenuate the autoimmune cascade in multiple sclerosis on the principal of antigen feeding. It may also be useful in treating some severe neurological symptoms of Lyme disease, which can closely resemble multiple sclerosis. **Recommended dosage:** 500 to 1,000 mg 2 to 3 times daily.
- *Glucosamine sulfate* is a substance naturally present in joint cartilage, and has been proposed as a therapy for arthritis. **Recommended dosage:** 500 to 1,000 mg 2 to 3 times daily.

REHABILITATION

Physical rehabilitation is essential to treatment and recovery from late-stage Lyme. People who are suffering from chronic Lyme disease are physically stopped in their tracks. They cannot exercise because of pain and fatigue. In fact, they often cannot even move about normally, and may spend much time bedridden. Muscles waste away, and joints may become swollen and damaged with arthritis, or simply stiffened from lack of use. Chronic Lyme weakens all of the body functions, organs and systems that are sustained and toned by exercise. The heart muscle itself can be weakened, and the immune system compromised by lack of exercise. There are metabolic changes too: most patients gain weight, put on extra fat, and suffer a worsening of the ratio of "good" HDL cholesterol to "bad" LDL cholesterol. There is increased risk of cardiovascular disease and diabetes. Any treatment of advanced Lyme disease must include a healthy diet and physical rehabilitation to restore the whole body to health.

First of all, it's important to ease into exercise. People who are under treatment for late stage Lyme really need rest and recuperation, and should not be trying to push themselves beyond their limited capacity. Physical and emotional stress will undermine effective treatment and healing.

When symptoms start to improve, it is possible to begin a very gentle program of physical therapy, preferably with the help of a trained professional therapist. The first stage of therapy may involve a whole range of techniques to relieve muscle spasms and soreness, including massage, heat therapy, ultrasound, and the like. These can be followed by light stretching and manipulation of joints to increase their range of motion. It's important not to move too quickly or push up against the pain threshold. The goal is to reduce soreness, reduce joint pain, and improve sleep patterns.

The second stage can include more stretching and some light muscular strengthening. It's important to proceed gradually and gently, so as not to further damage weakened joints and tendons. Gradually, patient and therapist can work toward aerobic exercise, working on all parts of the body. All therapy should include a gradual warm-up, and cool-down and stretches after exercise.

Psychological Support

Many of the early victims of Lyme disease had their symptoms dismissed as psychosomatic, and were told to seek psychotherapy. It's now known that the disease can physically attack the central nervous system, including the brain, and cause a whole range of neurological symptoms, including depression, memory loss, confusion, sleeplessness, even mild dementia.[5] We now treat these by treating for the disease itself, using diet, nutrient supplements and physical therapy to restore the body to health.

Still, the experience of long, debilitating illness, with pain and mental symptoms, puts a heavy strain on the spirit. Many victims of Lyme disease have turned to Lyme support groups. In these groups, members can not only share information about the latest developments in treatment and diagnosis, but can simply share feelings and experiences about living with the illness, undergoing treatment, and so on. Research into the mind-body connection with other diseases has shown that participating in this kind of support group can reduce anxiety and discomfort and actually improve outcomes. Most Lyme disease clinics and hospitals in endemic areas can refer patients to local support groups. See the RESOURCES section at the end of this booklet for more information on contacting Lyme support groups.

ALTERNATIVE TREATMENTS

There are several promising alternative treatments for Lyme disease that may prove beneficial with further research. One of these involves a technique similar to the desensitization therapy that allergists currently use. Allergies are caused by an overactive immune response to allergens, which might be anything from grass pollen to bee venom. The allergens are in themselves harmless, but the excessive immune reaction can cause discomfort, chronic illness, or even death. Desensitization, or immunotherapy, involves giving the patient small amounts of the allergy-causing substance by injection. This often causes the immune system to become accustomed to the material, so that it stops overreacting.

There are those who believe that this technique can help with Lyme disease, especially chronic Lyme disease that may involve an immune system imbalance. There are several practitioners in the U.S. who are using this, mostly environmental physicians, who are members of the American Academy of Environmental Medicine. They use a small amount of *Borrelia* antigen—not the whole organism, but fragments of it—to try to neutralize an overactive immune response to the spirochete.

Another experimental treatment also seems to work through the immune response, and is based on a procedure in veterinary medicine. To prevent disease, technicians inject killed germs into the udder of a cow before it calves. They then take the first milk that comes after the birth of a calf (called colostrum), and process it into whey, so that it will keep. The theory is that the cow will develop an immune defense, transmissible in the whey, that can be used to cure the original disease. Some have experimented with using killed Lyme spirochetes, "processing" them through a cow, and using the whey to treat human subjects, with positive results. Both of these procedures are innovative approaches to treating the immunological consequences of chronic Lyme, and require further study.

ADVANCED LYME: THE HOLISTIC APPROACH

In my own practice, I have treated several patients with late stage Lyme. The following example illustrates some of the complexities of diagnosis and treatment. I have found it essential to treat advanced Lyme holistically, that is attending to the multiple factors that may be causing symptoms in addition to the Lyme spirochete. Equally important, my goal in healing is not just to knock out a bug with antibiotic therapy, but also to bring about a transformation of lifestyle that will lead to true health and recovery.

LYME DISEASE MASQUERADING AS CHRONIC FATIGUE SYNDROME

Jerry was an active young lawyer who came to me when he was 32 years old, after suffering for six years from a very puzzling and distressing syndrome. Every three months, like clockwork, he would be hit by a debilitating exhaustion that sent him to his bed for three to ten days. He'd have occasional night sweats, but no fever, and would suffer from sore throat, headaches and body aches. In between he was fine, except for some residual low back pain. But this had been going on for *six years*.

Jerry had been under the care of a highly-respected immunologist who diagnosed him with chronic fatigue syndrome (CFS). Jerry came to me because of my experience in treating CFS, so I accepted this diagnosis at face value and started treatment with intravenous vitamin C. However, I also took a careful medical history. Jerry mentioned that he had had mononucleosis in college, and although he had recovered completely, a few years later he developed a "mono-like illness," with headache, low back pain, sinus pain, drowsiness and exhaustion. This developed into the recurring series of episodes described above, knocking him out every three months.

Even though I began treating him for CFS, this struck me as an atypical manifestation. The way he was cyclically ill, with such regularity, suggested some sort of life cycle of a virus or parasite. I decided to run some additional tests, and going down my check list, I asked if he'd ever been tested for Lyme. He hadn't, so we got some tests underway. Meanwhile, he showed no improvement from the CFS treatment I was giving him; his episodes of fatigue kept recurring.

When the ELISA test results came back, Jerry showed positive for Lyme. That could indicate exposure to Lyme, but didn't necessarily mean that active Lyme disease was causing his symptoms, and he wasn't showing any of the typical arthritic or neurological symptoms. His main symptom was that terrible weakness and something like the flu without a fever. So I did a Western blot test and it came back clearly positive, too. This was a pretty good indication that Lyme disease could be involved.

So I started Jerry on a trial of oral antibiotics, amoxicillin and probenacid, for six weeks. (We often use probenacid along with an antibiotic to keep a higher concentration of antibiotic in the body tissues.) I also gave him a basic nutrient package, including intravenous vitamin C, followed by oral doses, a basic multivitamin, plus a zinc supplement, acidophilus, and a magnesium supplement to help treat his fatigue. And I put him on a good healthy diet, low in sugar and refined carbohydrates, with plenty of whole grains and vegetables.

At first he felt slightly worse from the antibiotics, a typical reaction, but then Jerry definitely improved. And for the first time, he didn't have a recurrence of symptoms at the three-month point. When we repeated the ELISA test, it came back much lower, below the cutoff point for a positive Lyme indication.

Jerry seemed fine, but about six months later, he reported a slight return of the fatigue and malaise. This kind of return of symptoms after treatment is not uncommon in advanced Lyme disease. We checked him again for Lyme, and the test was negative. I made sure he was keeping up with the nutrient supplements and took another look at his general life-style. It turned out that he had let his diet slip, and was consuming a lot of sugar via desserts and fruit juices. We weaned him from those again, and he improved.

About a year after the initial antibiotic therapy, the symptoms returned. We treated him with the same antibiotic regimen as before, and he felt better for about six months, when the symptoms reappeared once again. This time I treated Jerry with a different oral antibiotic, Suprax. Two years have passed and he has been free of symptoms ever since.

Jerry's case holds some interesting lessons:

- Jerry had had no special risk factors. He'd visited the beach at East Hampton a couple of times. He'd gone bicycling in the country. But he had no recollection of any tick bite, any connection of his "mono-like" illness to a specific place or activity.
- He had none of the "classical" indicators for Lyme: aching joints, arthritic knees; Bell's palsy; neurological problems resembling meningitis or encephalitis; certainly not any rash that he remembered after six years. His primary symptom was the extreme fatigue and malaise which kept recurring in that cyclical way.
- Diet and nutrients were a basic part of Jerry's treatment, and his lingering symptoms would wax and wane depending on how conscientious he was with this part of his therapy.

What conclusions can we draw from Jerry's case? First, that we have to consider Lyme diagnostically even in the absence of apparent risk factors without the most typical symptoms. We have to consider extreme fatigue as a possible indicator for Lyme, while it is at the same time an indicator for other conditions such as CFS. And we should be on the lookout for symptoms that disappear and return. It does seem that some patients find their symptoms wax and wane according to what may be some kind of replication cycle of the *Borrelia* spirochete. This is why many Lyme specialists recommend long courses of treatment to extend across the spirochete's periods of dormancy and inactivity.

It's worth noting that Jerry was actually in good physical condition with a strong immune system. Unlike many patients who have vague, lingering symptoms that affect multiple systems, he was basically healthy, except that every few months his immune system would mount a robust response to the presence of the spirochete, and he'd be laid low. Yet because of the strong immune response, the Lyme bacteria didn't penetrate his central nervous system or his joints, and cause the sort of chronic, persistent problems that we see in people with impaired immunity.

Since Jerry was mis-diagnosed as having CFS, the Lyme treatment led to complete recovery. However, we also see patients who really do have CFS plus Lyme disease, and these people are much harder to treat. I don't believe people with CFS and other immune-deficient problems are inherently more susceptible to Lyme disease, but they are more susceptible to a drawn-out, atypical, recurring and insidious course of the disease.

FUTURE TRENDS AND ISSUES

Public awareness of Lyme disease is burgeoning, matched only by the increase in number of reported cases, and the apparent spread of the carrier ticks beyond the endemic areas. We can expect political and economic pressures to continue to build as well, because of the high cost of treating advanced Lyme disease.

On the hopeful side, there are now several active trials of a human vaccine for Lyme disease. The vaccine is made of fragments of spirochetal protein, to avoid the risk of inducing Lyme disease by giving weakened or dead organisms. It will probably be a year or two before results from these trials are published.

It's been only a relatively few years since Lyme disease was identified, and even fewer since the *Borrelia* spirochete was discovered as its cause. We have learned much about the illness, but much remains to be learned about the organism itself, its interaction with various systems of the body, the mechanisms of the disease process, and the means of treatment. There may be exciting discoveries to be made about the curious similarities between the courses and effects of such illnesses as chronic fatigue syndrome, syphilis, Alzheimer's disease, multiple sclerosis, rheumatoid arthritis and Lyme disease. Unfortunately, some have suffered terribly, and continue to suffer, from inadequate diagnosis and treatment of Lyme disease. Increased public awareness should help us with prevention, and we must look to the research activities now underway to provide us with more effective prevention, diagnosis, and treatment in the near future.

RESOURCES

ORGANIZATIONS AND NEWSLETTERS

- Lyme Disease Foundation, Inc., 1 Financial Plaza, Hartford, Connecticut 06103, 203-525-2000.
- Lyme Disease National Hotline: 800-886-LYME (5963).
- Local Lyme disease support and informational groups can be found in many areas. The Lyme Disease Network of New Jersey, 908-390-5027, maintains a current listing of support groups. The Lyme Disease Network is also establishing a new computer network, called The National Lymenet, which will provide a current listing of support groups nationwide available 24 hours a day.
- The "Lyme Disease Update" is a nationwide monthly newsletter. Call or fax 1-812-471-1990 for more information.
- The Lyme Disease Electronic Mail Network publishes the

"LymeNet Newsletter" once every 10 to 15 days. This interactive newsletter contains timely news about the Lyme disease epidemic, including medical abstracts, treatment protocols, prevention information, and political happenings.

Books and Videos

- Lang, Denise with DeSilva, Derrick Jr. (M.D.), *Coping with Lyme Disease: A Practical Guide to Dealing with Diagnosis and Treatment.* New York, Henry Holt & Company, 1993.
- Stephen Nostrom's nationally syndicated "Lyme Borrelia Outreach" television program is distributing four videos to Lyme support groups: contact Stephen Nostrom, Lyme Borrelia Outreach, P.O. Box 496, Mattituck, NY 11952.

REFERENCES

1. "The Polymerase Chain Reaction In the Diagnosis of Lyme Neuroborreliosis" by Pachner AR; Delaney E, *Ann Neurol* 1993 Oct; 34 (4): 544–50.
   "Detection of Borrelia Burgdorferi DNA By Polymerase Chain Reaction in Synovial Fluid From Patients With Lyme Arthritis" by Nocton JJ; Dressler F; Rutledge BJ; Rys PN; Persing DH; Steere AC, *N Engl J Med* 1994; 330: 229–34.
   "The Polymerase Chain Reaction For The Detection of Borrelia Burgdorferi In Human Body Fluids by Liebling MR; Níshio MJ; Rodriguez A; Sigal LH; Jin T; Louie JS, of Division of Rheumatology, Harbor University of California, Los Angeles Medical Center. *Arthritis Rheum* 1993 May; 36 (5): 665–75.
2. "Treatment of Lyme Disease" *The Medical Letter* vol. 34, Issue 881, October 16, 1992.
3. "Certain Treatments Hinder Lyme Detection" by Jane E. Brody. *The New York Times*, December 1, 1988.
4. "Diagnostic Hints and Treatment Guidelines For Lyme Disease" by Joseph J. Burrascano, Jr., M.D. *Joseph J. Burrascano, Jr. M.D.*, 139 Springs Fireplace Road, East Hampton, N.Y. 11937, (516) 324-7337, Sixth edition, March 1992.
5. "Psychiatric Manifestations of Lyme Borreliosis," by Fallon B; Nields J; et al, *Journal of Clinical Psychiatry* 1993; 54 (7): 263–68.
   "The neuropsychiatric manifestations of Lyme borreliosis" by Fallon B; Nields J; et al., *Psychiatric Quarterly* 1992; 63 (1): 95–117.